3

WINGS

WINGS

DOVERPICTURA

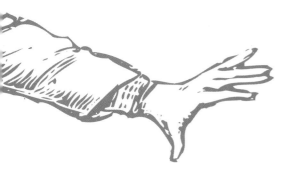

DOVER PUBLICATIONS, INC. | Mineola, New York

Planet Friendly Publishing
✔ Made in the United States
✔ Printed on Recycled Paper
 Text: 10% Cover: 10%
 Learn more: www.greenedition.org

GREEN EDITION

At Dover Publications we're committed to producing books in an earth-friendly manner and to helping our customers make greener choices.

Manufacturing books in the United States ensures compliance with strict environmental laws and eliminates the need for international freight shipping, a major contributor to global air pollution.

And printing on recycled paper helps minimize our consumption of trees, water and fossil fuels. The text of *Wings* was printed on paper made with 10% post-consumer waste, and the cover was printed on paper made with 10% post-consumer waste. According to Environmental Defense's Paper Calculator, by using this innovative paper instead of conventional papers, we achieved the following environmental benefits:

> **Trees Saved: 10 • Air Emissions Eliminated: 882 pounds**
> **Water Saved: 4,245 gallons • Solid Waste Eliminated: 258 pounds**

For more information on our environmental practices, please visit us online at www.doverpublications.com/green

By Alan Weller.
Designed by Joel Waldrep.

Wings is a new work, first published by Dover Publications, Inc., in 2010.

For permission to use more than ten images, please contact:
Permissions Department
Dover Publications, Inc.
31 East 2nd Street
Mineola, NY 11501
rights@doverpublications.com

The CD-ROM file names correspond to the images in the book. All of the artwork stored on the CD-ROM can be imported directly into a wide range of design and word-processing programs on either Windows or Macintosh platforms. No further installation is necessary.

ISBN 10: 0-486-99081-8
ISBN 13: 978-0-486-99081-1
Manufactured in the United States of America
Dover Publications, Inc., 31 East 2nd Street, Mineola, NY 11501
www.doverpublications.com

005

006

8

007 background

INTER OMNES.

Obtenebrat Stellas Phæbe; tu sola puellas: Pulcræ essent aliæ, tu nisi, pulcra fores.

008

011

012

013

015

016

017

018

020 background 019

13

021

022 background

023

024

025

026 background

028

030

031 background

032

033

034

035 background

19

037

038

036

039

041

042

043

044

047

050

051

052 background

055

057

058 background

056

059

060

061

062 background

065

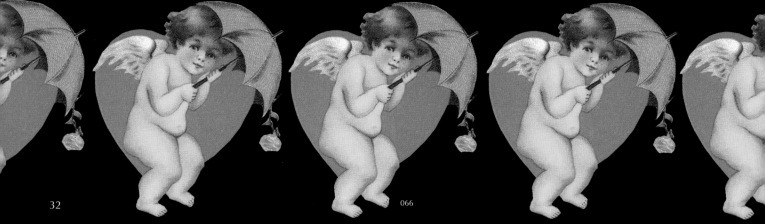

32

066

067

TRUE

LOVE

068

070

071

072

073

074

075

076

AU BON MARCHÉ

LE DERNIER CRI DE LA NAVIGATION AÉRIENNE.

078

079 background

080

081

082 background

083

084

085 background

086

087

088

089

090

091

092

093

094

40

095 background

096

097

098

099

101

102

103

104 background

MANUFACTURE ROUBAISIENNE

106

107

108

109 background

110

111

112

113 background

115

116

48

117

118

119

120

121 background

123

122

124

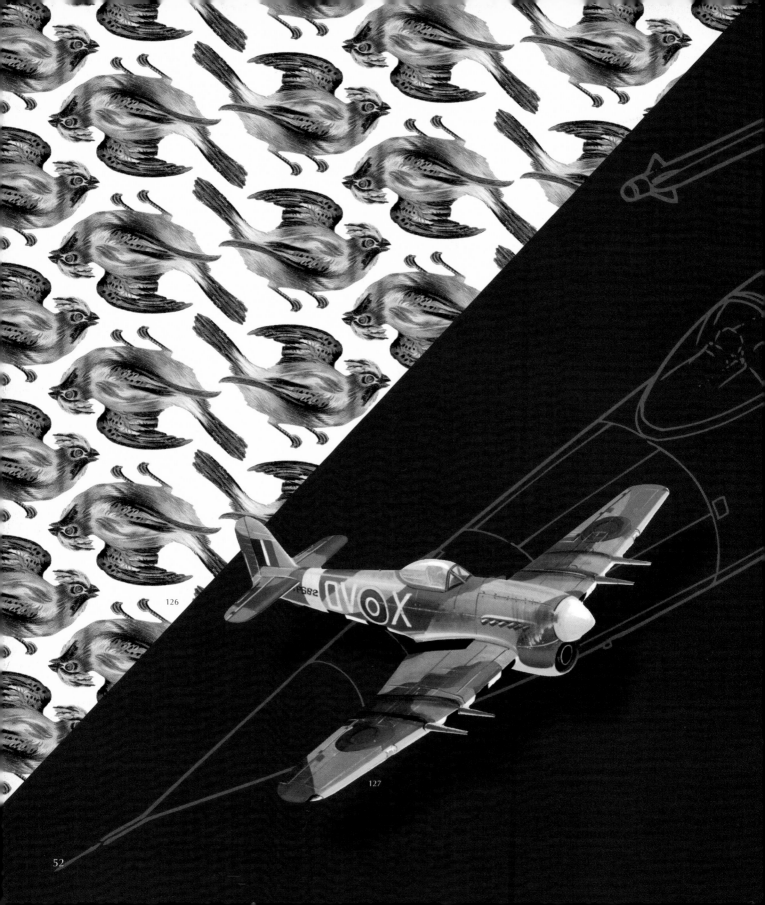

126

127

52

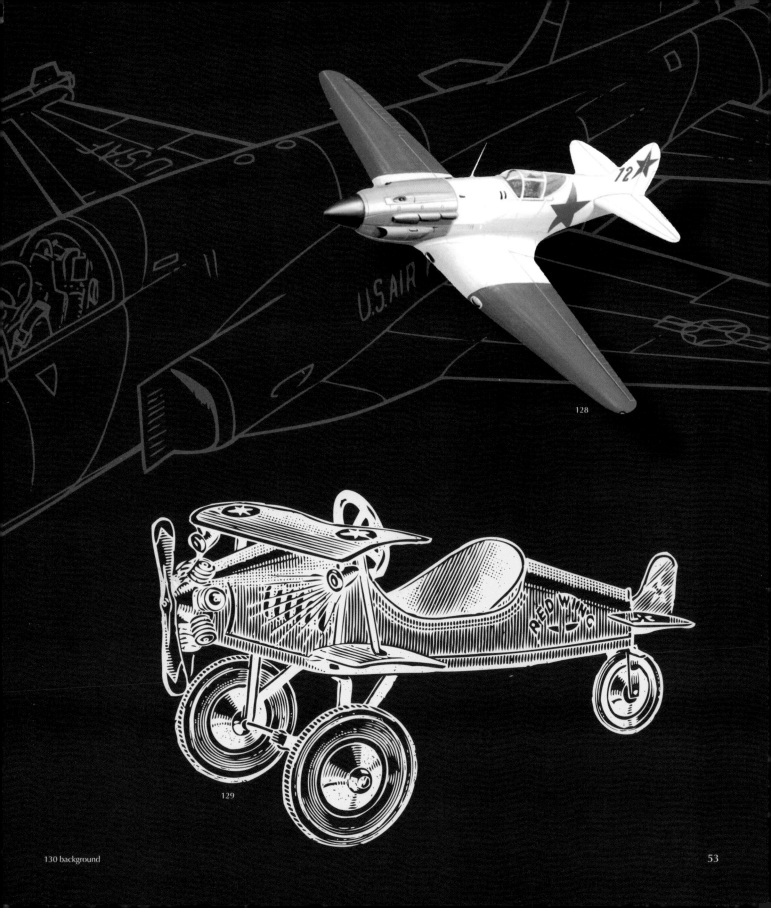

128

129

131

132

134

135

137

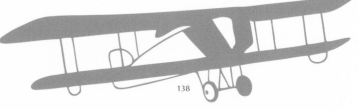

138

139

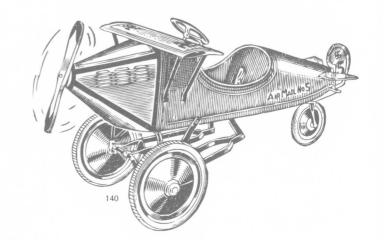

140

56

141

142

143

57

144

145

146

ARCTIC BYRD

147

150

151

152

153

154

155 background

157 background

158

159

160

161

162 background

165

166

167

168

169

AI-III

171

172

173

174

175 background

176

CHARLES LIVINGSTON BULL

178

179

180

182

183

184

185 background

186

187

188

189

190

191

192

194

195

196

197

198

199

200

201

202

203 background

204

205

206

207

208 background

209

210

211

212

213

215

216

217

220

221

222 background

226 background

225

227

229

232 background

230

231

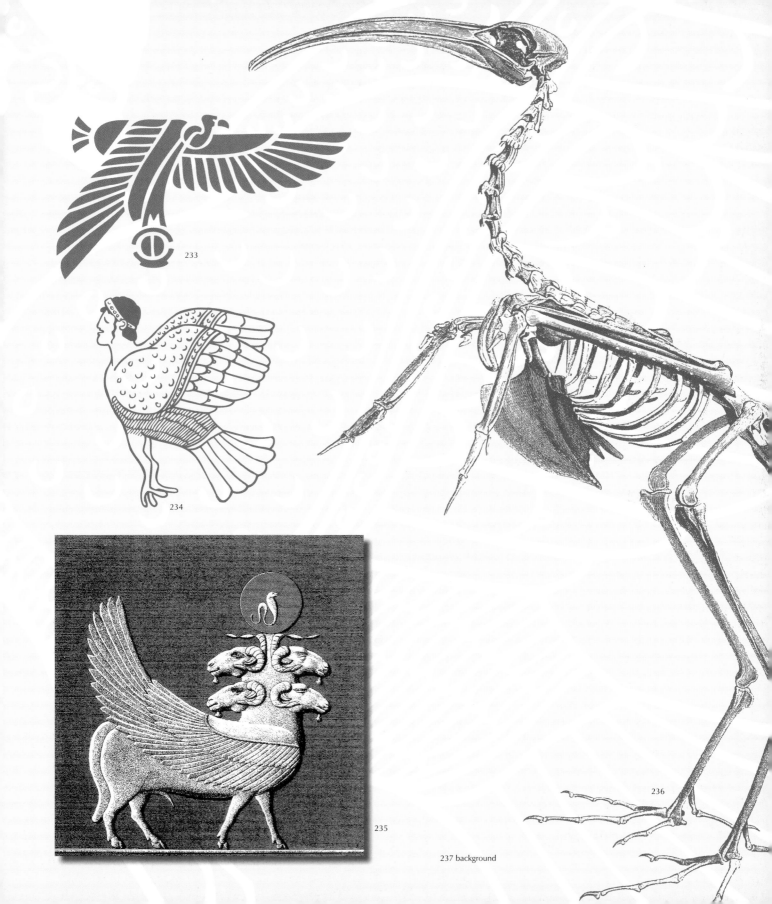

233

234

235

237 background

236

238

239

240

241

242

243

244

245

246 background

247

248

249

250 background

251

252

VAMPIRES OVERHEAD

254

256

257

258

259

260 background

263

264

265

266

267

272

276

277

278

279

280

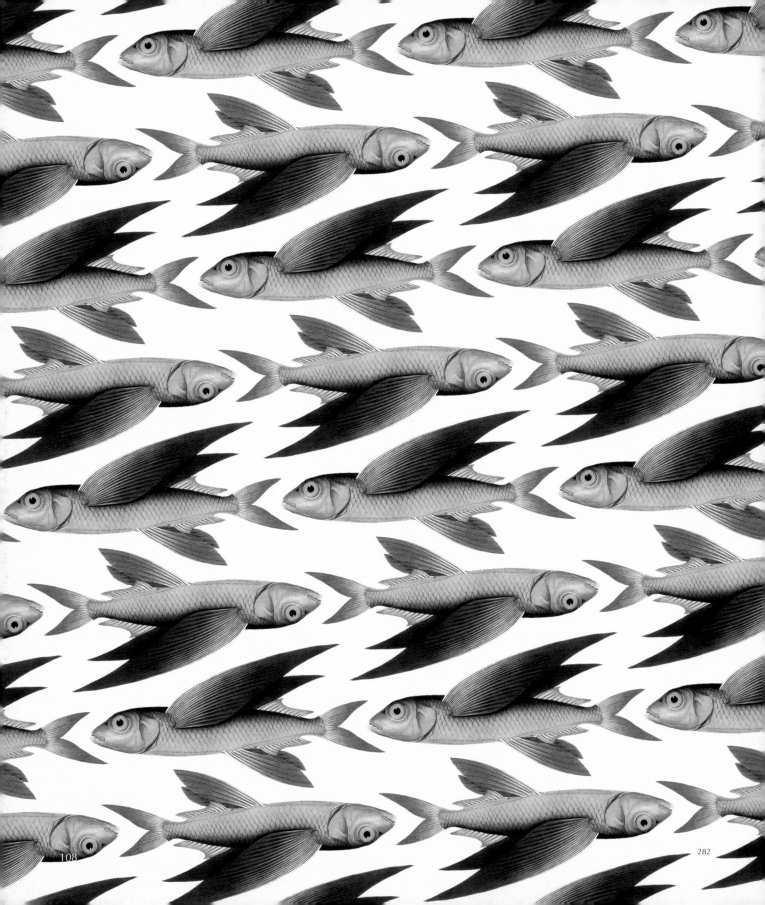

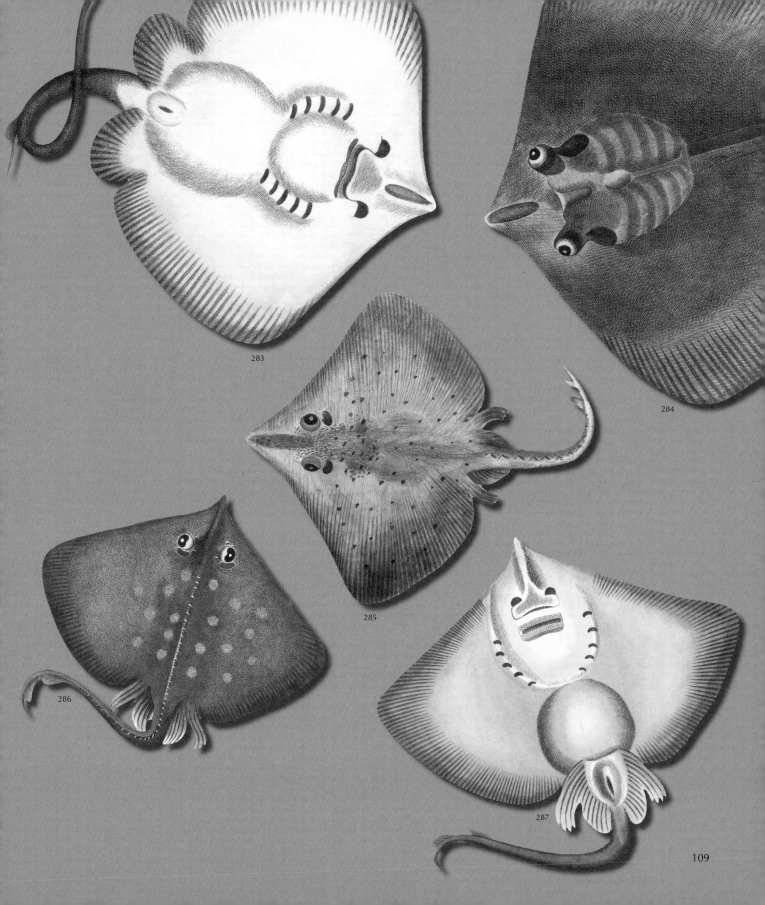

283

284

285

286

287

VI

Gli Amanti

XIV

la Temperanza

X

la Ruota della Fortuna

il Diavolo

288

289

290

291

292

110

294

295 background

G. Doré

H. PISAN

296

297

298

300

301

302

303

305

306

307

DEI · DONVM

308

310

311

312

314

315

316

317 background

120

318

319 background

121

320

321

122

322

323

325

326

327

328

329

330

VIRTUS IN ACTIONE CONSISTIT

331

332

333

334

335 background

List of Images

List of Vector Images